# 5 EASY STEPS TO CREATE YOUR OWN
# Authentic Home

## KATHY BANAK

Copyright © 2024 Kathy Banak
All rights reserved
First Edition

NEWMAN SPRINGS PUBLISHING
320 Broad Street
Red Bank, NJ 07701

First originally published by Newman Springs Publishing 2024

ISBN 979-8-89061-100-0 (Paperback)
ISBN 979-8-89061-102-4 (Hardcover)
ISBN 979-8-89061-101-7 (Digital)

Printed in the United States of America

To my loving parents who inspired me to create with loving kindness. To my posse of smart, strong, and sassy friends who graciously help me create my foundation. A special thanks to Emma and Connie for their wise literary insights and heartfelt encouragement. And to my husband, Rick, for his continuing love, unwavering support, and guidance to the light.

# INTRODUCTION

## MY JOURNEY

Growing up as a young girl in Connecticut, my mother, Mary, and I would spend hours in local fabric stores surrounded by a vast array of textures and colors in search of the perfect solution for our window coverings or clothing creations. She would spend countless hours creating seasonal decorative arrangements for our front door or planning her next home-re-decorating project. Our family's home had all the latest home décor trends, such as orange kitchen carpeting and shiny vinyl lime green and yellow plaid wallpaper, both of which were very popular back in the seventies.

My father's love of nature led him to become a successful landscape designer and tree farmer. My maternal grandmother, also Mary, displayed her love and creativity through her knitting and her baking of the best chocolate chip cookies. My paternal grandmother and great-aunt's appearances were very important to them as they were always impeccably dressed and never went out of the house without their beautifully colored hats that would rival any British socialite. My great aunt lived in a large home full of beautiful antiques, floor-to-ceiling draperies in every room, and huge beds made of down pillows and comforters that you could get lost in. It was a dream-like paradise for a young, impressionable girl who was always attracted to all things beautiful.

I often escaped the chaotic noise of my three brothers into a backyard home sanctuary. It was made from old barnboard and included two windows and a path that led to its front door. I spent countless hours decorating it with colorful paint, window coverings, and handmade furniture, and it became my home away from home. When acting in our neighborhood plays, I felt most comfortable creating the sets for each of its scenes. My father's and brothers' strong male energy developed my resilience and perseverance skills, which became especially apparent at the dinner table as I quickly had to gather food before there was nothing left. Growing boys consumed food without conversation, and it took everything within me to hunt and gather simply for my survival. My family's gifts are an integral part of my soul, and little did I know at the time that all these natural pulls of creating beautiful things would someday be at the heart of me today.

After college, I embarked on a career in sales in the fast-paced high-tech world, and I rode the wave for several years until I burned out from working with type-A personalities in the male-driven industry. A year of traveling provided me with a clear path to embark on a leap of faith to follow my intuition and relocate to the west coast. Moving to the breathtaking beauty of the Pacific Northwest provided me with a constant flow of inspiration and self-confidence, but that occasionally needed some nurturing. At times, I found myself crying to sleep often out of fear of the unknown, yet looking back, I now realize that my traditional upbringing and determination to be authentic to myself propelled me to walk through all my fears to get to the other side.

My first venture into remodeling was with the purchase of my first house a year after I arrived in Seattle. I hired a contractor and immediately turned a dated 1940s bungalow into a functional and aesthetically pleasing home both inside and out. I added a second-floor dormer, gutted an unfunctional kitchen, and designed both front and backyard gardens that brought joy to many. Full of firsthand remodeling experience, I was ready to take on the world with my newly felt enthusiasm and confidence.

Once settled in my new home, a neighbor asked me to help her redo her living room, and I felt that this call was the universe pushing me onto a design path. I selected new living room and hallway paint colors and rearranged the furniture pieces conducive for conversations. For much-needed privacy, I installed inexpensive draperies on the large front windows and relocated artwork throughout the house. The changes provided new energy to the house, and my neighbor was thrilled with the results. Her excitement and encouragement for my design adventure led her to host a party for me. She graciously showcased her new home and me as her interior designer. I was now on my way.

When you learn to color as a child, you learn to stay within the lines. That was what we were taught, and it was "the rule." I lived by the rules my whole life, up until my move to Seattle in my late thirties. I was way out of my line, and at times, I felt very uneasy and unsure of what I was doing. My fears of "what if it doesn't work out" were slowly silenced by the "what if I don't try" feelings, which eventually overtook me. My determination and faith provided me with the groundswell to overcome my self-doubt and embrace a new way of living my life.

What better way to really see what I was made of than to move clear across the country by myself into the unknown. The ebbs and flows of my career and personal life had planted my seeds of creativity and belief in trusting the universe. I slowly realized that my soul was wired with both female and male energies that I easily could switch between. It was with my inner knowingness to continue trusting in the universe and myself that I uncovered, through coaching and interior design classes, that I was on a new career and self-discovery path.

After several intuitive visions, which always seem to occur for me while in my shower, I felt the desire to create a place for people seeking guidance with paint colors, fabrics, and home furnishing selections. But first, I needed a business name. After weeks of trying to decide on a name, I went within, and my inner voice nudged me to invite several lady friends and colleagues over to my home for a naming party. I made sure that all the invitees were from various backgrounds and careers so that I could get the best out of our brainstorming session. On three-by-five-inch cards, I wrote words that resonated with me and were related to interior design and home décor and scattered all over my coffee table. I asked everyone to mix and match the cards to create a unique, impactful, and easily recognizable business name. When I paired the words *authentic* and *home*, I knew I had finally found my business name, my new career, and the beginning of my self-discovery.

Now that I realized I had a gift, a business name, and a burning desire to share it, it was time to execute. Authentic Home was born in the spring of 2003 after I remodeled a retail house into a design store that represented a Northwest boutique paint line that we mixed in the basement. I created my own private-label fabric line and sold a variety of home accessories. My design team assisted customers with selecting paint colors and facilitating their home projects, whatever they entailed. With the economic downturn in 2008 and my desire to work on my own client's projects instead of managing other designers, I relocated my business to a smaller storefront in the same town. This realignment of my retail business allowed me to design my own paint line with a local paint manufacturer. The sixty colors of the Authentic Home Color Paint were organized into five feeling or mood boards to make the paint color decision process easier. The store was passionate about assisting customers with the daunting paint color selection process, and we quickly became the talk of the community, with several appearances in the local media.

For several years, I ventured into the full-time deep abyss of online dating which finally led me to find and marry my husband at age fifty-five. Yet another example of my faith is trusting the universe's timing and I'll talk more about marrying later in life in my next book! Throughout the year and a half of dating, Rick and I continued down the remodeling path and flipped both his former home, where he raised his two daughters, and his childhood home.

Prior to our engagement, Rick decided to plant roots in a suburb where he found a lot with a small view of Puget Sound and decided to build his first house. This was his house, his budget, and I was his interior designer whose role was to advise and recommend materials to achieve his goal of a traditional rustic house. Midway through the build, we got engaged and finished the house and then I moved in. A year after our wedding, life took us on a new path and we moved to the golf resort community an hour east of Seattle.

We purchased a fourteen-year-old house and readily took on yet another remodeling project. For some crazy reason, the house had five different types of flooring throughout which I immediately changed to one midtone-engineered hardwood floor solution. The new minimal paint color palette that covered the dark and tired interior doors and trims lightened up all the walls throughout the house. These two projects alone drastically changed the entire look and feel of the house, yet we didn't stop there. We removed five windows and doors that were incorrectly placed and updated a craftsman-style stair railing to a modern cable rail system for the second-floor bedroom and loft area. It was not a small undertaking, and the result was pure happiness in our home.

We all experienced our unforgettable 2020 pandemic, which propelled most of us to be in our homes 24-7 as we lived, worked, and played indoors. Many of us had the time to clean out and organize spaces that we've been putting off for years, created new work-from-home spaces, shopped online for new home goods, or painted our kitchen cabinets. The pandemic forced us to be in our houses, which shed light on how we were living within their four walls. Hopefully, some of us have made positive changes to our physical surroundings. Yet for many of us, the pandemic was a challenging time, and many felt stuck.

Rick's job promotion and the local booming real estate market were some of our incentives to relocate once again and we chose the beautiful Coeur d' Alene, Idaho, to call home. We purchased a modest house in the spring of 2022, and we were fueled with our creative juices to once again transform the house into our home for decades to come. A new paint color palette, a new kitchen, new flooring, and the removal of doors, windows, and walls were all on the project list, and my role as the general contractor was a top priority. During this time, I also moved my elderly parents into an assisted living facility, and my perseverance took hold again for me to complete all the tasks on my plate. After months of decision-making and moving, I am pleased that everyone is now settled and loving our new homes.

With the hectic year behind me, I now had the time to take a deep breath and process what is next for me and my career. I could see and feel a design path of some kind, yet I didn't have a flashlight or the ability to clearly define what it was. Until my inner voice and constant external visual questions guided me to birth this book for you. I've rediscovered a lovely sitting chair in my office decorated in a fun polka-dot fabric that is now my quiet-time chair, and I spend time meditating, journaling, and writing in it.

I encourage you to find your "lovely sitting chair" or cozy corner space in- or outside your home for your quiet time, as we all need time to nourish and feed our souls.

## The Meaning of Authentic Home

*Authentic home* are two words that have individual meanings, yet when combined, they convey something much more profound. *Merriam-Webster's* definition of *authentic* means real or genuine: not copied, false, or fake; true to one's own personality, spirit, or character. *Home* is defined as one's place of residence, a familiar or usual setting. When one is "at home," the word resonates with being relaxed and comfortable, in harmony with one's surroundings.

*Authentic home* means finding your own voice so you can create a home that represents your true self, your authentic self. It is about being true to your own spirit and your family and sharing that with everyone who enters your front door. The craziness of the world we live in nowadays can easily overwhelm us and overtake our lives, and now, more than ever, we need to have a home that provides us with comfort and peace and is a place to restore one's soul.

My intuitive knowingness and vision are the skills I utilize when I am asked to help clients with their home's interiors. My goal in sharing my design, color, and spiritual insights is to inspire you to live authentically and to be aware of the amazing energy of your personal and physical surroundings. Any time you begin a remodeling project, paint a room, or simply rearrange furniture, it's a time of transformation, not only of the physical space but also of the spirit of your home and yourself.

I believe wholeheartedly that clients contact me when the time is right and that they are ready for not only their house's transformation but also their own transformation. We all strive to create and live in a beautiful home environment—an environment that is quiet, peaceful, calm, organized, and filled with an abundance of positive, healthy energy within the interior and around the exterior. And there is a definite connection between personal and physical energy, and it is very powerful to be aware of and be part of both. They are connected, and the more you live in an aesthetically pleasing home and feed good positive energy into it, the more you will get back from it.

Do you love your home and feel at peace in it? Is your home a true representation of yourself and your family? Are you in harmony with your home? If you answer yes to these questions, wonderful! You understand the powerful connection between one's home and one's spirit. If you are unsure or answered no to the questions, then think about what you don't like about your home and why.

My passion is to guide you on the path of creating a home you love that represents you and your family and not someone else. I view my role as a facilitator of energy, a home therapist and healer, and you will now have the framework to embark on your new authentic path. These steps are tools to help you see and feel your home in a new light and inspire you to transform it into your own *authentic home*. I am very grateful that I can be part of the transformation of not just one spirit but many, as the change affects everyone in a home, from you to the kids to the family pets. Enjoy the journey!

# CHAPTER 1

# DISCOVER THE SOUL OF YOUR HOUSE

### Be a Guest in Your Own House

Stand inside by your front door, close your eyes, relax, and then open your eyes. What are the first things you see, and how do you feel? Do you see a closet door or a long hallway that leads to sliding doors and outside through the backyard? Or do you see clutter spread all over the living room and immediately feel anxious? Everyone wants to have an aesthetically pleasing experience and feel positive energy upon entering a home through the front door, and it's important to decide what you want to see and how you want to feel when you first enter your house.

One of my pet peeves is when an interior front door aligns directly with a back sliding or French door that leads to a back porch or backyard. While you stand at the front door, you see all the way through the house and into the backyard, and so the energy comes through the front door and goes directly through the entire house and right outside. Why would you want to have all the energy leave your house right when you walk inside? A simple solution is to place distractors in front of the energy's path to distract or stop it and allow it to then stay within the house. Some examples of distractors or stops are the use of green-potted plants, a chandelier, a furniture grouping, or a screen that will deter energy from leaving your home. The goal is to have a welcoming and inviting experience for you and your guests to enter and for all the energy to stay in your home.

## Feel and See Your House

I've experienced the interiors of hundreds of homes over the years and witnessed all kinds of ways in which people live inside them. And I sense that many are unaware of their physical surroundings, but they don't have a sense of how their house feels, and they are stuck in a particular way of living their lives in their houses.

Early in my design career, I was intrigued by the art of feng shui and hired a consultant to visit my first home. The time we shared was a quick course to understanding the principles of art and the importance of energy flow within a home environment. After our session, I was pleasantly surprised to learn that my newly remodeled home had positive energy, and I chalked it up to my intuitive ability to feel my home.

Feng shui is an ancient Chinese metaphysical art that works with the unseen forces the ancients called "the breath of cosmic life" or chi. Chi, or energic force, is the life force that powers all living organisms. The literal translation for the word *feng* is wind and *shui* is water, and in Chinese culture, both words are associated with good health. It is the art of arranging buildings, objects, and space in an environment to achieve harmony and balance. To strengthen our life force, we need to improve the quality and amount of positive energy in our environment. You cannot begin to activate and manifest change in your life until you improve the chi that is already in your home. Feng shui focuses on nurturing the chi by correcting, adjusting, and enhancing the homes we live in to improve the flow of energy.

If hiring a feng shui consultant is not your thing, then take some time to get a sense of how our physical house feels. Quiet yourself and try to get a sense of how the energy of the house feels when you enter through your front and back doors. Do you feel a sense of warmth and happiness or cool chaos? Energy is associated with every element within your house, and you may love how your house feels right now. That is fantastic that you've achieved a feeling that aligns with yourself. Or perhaps this is the first time you've thought about the energy or feeling of your house, and congratulations, you've become aware of the first step. Feeling your house is an important first step in understanding its energy. Getting in touch with one's feelings may be difficult for some, but it is important to consider it when you want to make changes to how you live in your home.

Just as it is important to feel your house, it's also important to take time and inventory what you see when you walk through the front door or back door. Do you see an organized and aesthetically pleasing living room and kitchen? Or do you see a cluttered entry or dining room with papers and toys? A chaotic room full of clutter can cause anxiety and stress and have a negative impact on one's mood. Remember, an organized home is the framework for an organized mind.

Take the time to keep each room clutter-free and organized, and you're your mood will improve! Make a list of what you feel and see, and then work on simple solutions to change a negative space into a positive one. A transformation can't be achieved without knowing what it is that you want to change.

Earlier in my design career, I realized that the paint selection process was a frustrating task and often can be very emotional. This understanding became very evident to me when I was hired by a woman for a color consultation. As I walked into her home, I was bowled over by the bright Pepto-Bismol pink color on the living and dining room walls. It took me several minutes to see the baby grand piano in the corner because of the overbearing pink color. I inquired as to how long the paint color had been on the walls, and she sheepishly said ten years, and I couldn't believe that she and her family lived with this color for a decade. She knew by the look on my face that I was shocked and ready to get started when I suddenly realized that her entire dining room table was covered with paint chips of many different colors from several different paint manufacturers. She had been searching for the right paint colors for over six months and finally realized she needed help and mustered up the courage to call me.

I had such sadness in my heart when I realized that this woman and her family were really not only stuck with selecting paint colors but also emotionally stuck with the inability to feel or see her house, and the strong pink color stopped them in their tracks from seeing everything else in the room. She shared her new home's desires, and within minutes, I created a new color palette for the entire main floor. The new paint colors enhanced the hardwood floors, furniture, artwork, and accessories throughout the main floor. Upon leaving, I realized that the emotion of our time together was a lot for her, and she suddenly burst into tears. She told me they were tears of joy, and we both were relieved that, finally, she had a new direction for her home and a new path forward for her life. I was able to envision an outcome at the right time so her own transformation could begin.

## Envision Your New Home

One of the reasons many get overwhelmed when thinking about starting a home remodeling project is the overwhelming amount of material choices available today. There are literally thousands of styles and finishes of cabinetry, tiles, lighting, plumbing fixtures, furniture, fabrics, and paint colors to choose from. And all are available at your fingertips online or at national retail stores.

The explosion of *HGTV* design shows, Instagram, Pinterest, Houzz, and various home décor blogs has fueled our desires to live in aesthetically beautiful and finished homes. Yet the reality is that many of us don't have unlimited budgets and an army of craftspeople at our beck and call to design us a new kitchen or build us our dream home. Even a "simple" bathroom remodeling involves the process of selecting and designing all the tiles and selecting the cabinetry, countertop material, and plumbing and lighting fixtures, and it is simply overwhelming for many.

The vast number of material choices available today and all the decisions that need to be made on time add to your stress, and frustration sets in. We are bombarded with beautiful home interior images, which set our expectations high for our continued research and analysis of the perfect solution. This hamster wheel of ongoing research can be exhausting.

Thankfully, nowadays, there are plenty of online tools like Pinterest boards and Houzz ideabooks you can create and use to visualize your finished project. I encourage clients to save images of every detail of a project, whether it's bathroom tiles in one image or the finish of pendant lights in another. All the visuals are important to gather during the initial project phase and save for inspiration throughout the project and for future reference.

To keep your vision alive throughout the process, I encourage you to keep all the project specifics organized and easily accessible. I continually reference client Houzz ideabooks or Pinterest boards throughout the project to ensure that all the project decisions are in alignment with your intended look and feel.

Designers have various tools they utilize during initial client meetings to conceptualize what they want to achieve with the look and feel of a project. When I am working with a new client, I have both the client and I create Houzz ideabooks, and we use the visuals to discuss the project specifics. The overall paint color palette direction and the styles and finishes of materials such as cabinetry, lighting, plumbing fixtures, hardware, and fabrics are outlined, and we all have a path that is clearly defined to follow.

Houzz ideabooks can easily be accessed through the Houzz phone app, which can be used throughout the project for encouragement when you feel the urge to divert off the path. If you prefer a tactile tool, I recommend using magazine images of items that you resonate with. Tear out images of anything you resonate with and keep them organized in a binder for reference and inspiration. Visuals help to clarify how you want your space to look and are an important tool with which to start any project. Keep your visuals close by and refer to them throughout your project for continued inspiration. Regularly review your Houzz ideabooks, Pinterest boards, or magazine images and communicate your vision with your team. A clear vision of your project, whatever the size, will help you stay on track and achieve your desired outcome.

Try not to get caught up with style categories such as traditional, transitional, contemporary, farmhouse modern, rustic, or industrial. For some of your DIYers out there, these guidelines may help you focus on finding your own "style" to achieve your goal. But for many, it can be confusing to have to stay within "an expert's" definition that relates to a specific design style. Define your own style and stay within you. Don't ask too many friends or family for their opinions about your home and your style. Remember, it's about you and your authenticity, not someone else's.

Now that we have a vision for our home outline, how do you want your space to feel? How do you want others to feel in your space? As I evolve and become more in tune with myself, I notice how my emotions and feelings are affected by my surroundings. Have you ever walked into someone's home and immediately felt a warm, comfortable feeling? Or have you experienced a cold, distant feeling while in another home? What colors of clothing do you gravitate toward, and what feelings do you have when you wear them?

I physically feel a change within my body when I am in a chaotic room painted in a bright color versus how I feel in a beautiful room decorated in serene soft colors of blues and greens. I feel differently when I wear my favorite red dress, as red portrays a feeling of energy and excitement. You might know that you gravitate toward warm-based colors versus cool-based colors just by how you react to them and how they make you feel. The data has been around for decades, outlining the correlation between color and the effect it has on one's moods, and more on this is in chapter 3. Staying true to the feelings and vision you want to achieve will aid in alleviating the added stress and frustration of your project.

## Commit to Your Vision

My goal is to provide you with a roadmap for your project's completion. The tools outlined in this book are designed to make it easy for you to find your vision and execute a plan to completion. Once you've decided on your project, however big or small, stay committed to seeing it through to the end. I've watched projects start with excitement and then stop halfway through because of unforeseen circumstances. We all have curveballs and disruptions that come into our lives, and the key is to get back on the path as soon as possible and complete the project. Prioritize what is important to you and your project, and then commit to making it happen. And just like my perseverance skills that were developed with my brothers at the kitchen table, your commitment and determination are necessary ingredients to complete your transformation.

# Chapter 2

# GET YOUR JOURNEY STARTED

Is your living room calling you for a new paint color, or is your master bathroom in need of a refresh? Is the layout of your mudroom not working for you and your family? Decide on the project you want to tackle, define its scope, and then outline the next steps you need to take to get started. Start with a small project first, especially if you are intimidated by the overwhelming number of material choices available today and if you have a hard time making decisions.

## Value Your Time

For all the DIYers who don't consider that your time is valuable and think you will save money by not hiring a professional, then think again. Everyone has an hourly rate whether you are a do-it-yourselfer or a professional, and it needs to be considered when deciding on who is going to perform the physical labor of the project. Yes, you have an hourly rate just like a subcontractor. To calculate your estimate, include the time you think it will take you to finish the project and then triple the amount of time.

My experience has shown me that life has a funny way of coming up and distracting DIYers from finishing a project. Also include all the material costs that you need to purchase for the project. Now you can compare apples to apples between your estimate and a professional's estimate, and I recommend getting at least two professional trade estimates. Wouldn't you rather play outside on a summer weekend than work on your home project indoors? And if you work full-time, do you want to work on the weekends on your home project? Once you realize what your time is worth, you are now ready to compare the professional estimates to your own. It's important to value your time when making this important decision.

A budget is dependent on the size and scope of the project, and it needs to be discussed and finalized prior to starting. We all have experienced either our own project or someone else's who starts a project with a budget, and within weeks, the budget is gone, and either the project stops or it continues without knowing how much it will cost to finish. The stress of not knowing can be alleviated with regular budget check-ins with yourself, your partner, and your contractor. Most of us want to know what something costs before starting. I still have some clients who never outline a budget for me to work with, and this is not the norm for most of us.

## Your Team

Clients come into my life when they need help on a project and when they realize they don't have the bandwidth or desire to take on a project from beginning to end. If you don't have the skills to design a kitchen or bathroom, select and order all the project materials, lay out furniture and lighting, and manage the project and all the subcontractors, then it's time to create a team of professionals who will achieve your project's vision and goals.

Whether it's a handyman, painter, electrician, plumber, or general contractor expertise you need for your project, it is best to do your homework beforehand and start with referrals from family and friends. Most of us have done or are planning to do a remodel project and getting a referral from a source you know, and trust is a great way to begin. If you've just moved into a new neighborhood and don't know of any trade professionals, your realtor is a great source for referrals, or consult online resources like Nextdoor or Angie's List. Always check several references, and listen to your intuition before making your final decision. Whether you like it or not, when you take on your DIY project or hire a professional contractor or subcontractor like a painter, you must become your own general contractor. It is your house you are transforming with their help. You're the leader of your destiny and your house transformation.

If a painting is your next project, I encourage you to hire a professional painter to do the work. A professional painter on your team will be the most efficient and cost-effective way to begin living in your freshly painted house. A painter's job is to paint, and they will arrive at your house equipped with all the materials and equipment needed to get the project done. You may have loved painting years ago, but now your life has changed, and you have other priorities. Also take into consideration all the paint equipment and supplies that are needed for the project if you plan on doing the work. Depending on the scope of the project, these supplies, in addition to the cost of all the paint, will add to your overall budget. Value your time and your desire to complete the project sooner rather than later.

# Organization

In our family, I am the designer, leader, organizer, project manager, and eternal optimist, and simply said, I get things done. Not every family has one person with all these skill sets, and it's best to hire a professional who has the skills to complement yours. And having someone who is organized is important to be a part of your team. I've partnered with very disorganized contractors and caused unnecessary delays, and they were never hired again. Don't assume all general or subcontractors are organized, and it's important that you keep track of every aspect of your project. There are estimates, material specifications, invoices, and receipts that need to stay organized—not just for ordering purposes but also for future reference.

When I am hired to select all the materials for a new construction project, I must keep organized from the research phase to the finalized decisions so that all the materials get ordered correctly, arrive on time, and then installed correctly. I use a project notebook for the day-to-day to-do lists and a small file bin for eight-by-eleven-inch file folders arranged by project, such as flooring, paint colors, plumbing fixtures, estimates, and invoices. For large remodels or new construction projects, I use a detailed project specification spreadsheet that evolves as the project evolves. These tools help you stay organized and focused on the tasks at hand. I often reference my file bins months after a project is completed for specific measurements or color and fabric samples. There are several online project management tools to research beforehand to find which tools work best for you.

And take into consideration the delays that most likely will occur with your project. Since the pandemic, we've all experienced severe supply chain delays that can add several months to the project timeline. One of my clients waited eleven months for a new light fixture, and our new counter stools were ordered ten months ago, and they just arrived. All remodel projects experience delays, with most being out of our control. Hiring reliable professionals who regularly show up on time, overcome weather disruptions, and adjust to materials shipment delays will all impact a project's timeline. Set realistic expectations for your project, and expect that hiccups will occur. Take a deep breath, and remember that this, too, shall pass.

# Clean Out and Declutter

Have you ever visited a home full of clutter, and nothing is in its place? How did it make you feel? There have been several times clients have wanted to partner with me on a project, and I couldn't work with them because the minute I entered the home, I knew that they were not ready for me because of all the clutter everywhere my eyes could see. A house needs to be rid of clutter before any new project can begin, so start with a fresh slate so you can see what needs to be done.

An organized home provides the framework for an organized mind. If you find yourself holding on to "stuff" for a long time and realize that clutter has taken over your way of living in your house, an initial step is to read up on organizational methods. Online blogs and books are available today that outline steps for you to take to clear out and live with less "stuff."

One of the bestselling books a few years ago is *The Life-Changing Magic of Tidying Up* by Marie Kondo. The quick read outlines her methodology for getting rid of clutter and staying organized. There are many reasons people hold on to their "stuff" and continue to buy more "stuff." A simple rule of thumb to use is to disregard an item if you don't love it. If the item doesn't resonate with you, then it's time to get rid of it so someone else can enjoy it. If you've tried reading the organizational books and blogs and still find yourself falling back into your old habits of collecting "stuff," then consider partnering with a certified professional organizer or CPO. The National Association of Productivity and Organization Professional website and other local websites can direct you to find a professional in your community. It's important to clear out and get rid of things before you start a new home project.

For those of you who feel a sense of clarity and accomplishment with a good clean-out of your house, stay on track with semiannual clean-out days of your entire house, including the basement and garage. Garage sales and selling "stuff" online are great ways to clear out your spaces. Donation locations are in every community, and it makes you feel good when you donate some of your "stuff" to someone who can really use it. During all our recent moves, donating items we didn't want or need fulfilled us, knowing that our things were going to good use. Are your closets the catch-all for all of you and your family's "stuff"? Or is the mudroom the chaotic dumping space for everyone's "stuff"? Everyone's "stuff" is connected to energy, and the gathering and clearing out of the "stuff" provide a path for new energy to enter your home.

If your budget allows, I encourage you to partner with a professional custom closet company for all the interior closets as well as built-in organization in a mudroom, office, and garage. Once you move away from the standard wire rack closet systems to built-in closet cabinetry, it's like flying first class, and there is no going back to coach! Custom closets provide a lot more storage for your clothes, shoes, bags, and the like, as everything has a place to land and is organized.

    I've been recommending garage closets for some time now, and they are a great way to hide all the seasonal items, house paint, outdoor activity gear, tools, and gardening "stuff." It makes such a pleasant experience to enter an organized and aesthetically pleasing garage.

    With our recent remodeling, I partnered with a local California Closets team for our new master closet, and we transformed the once–wire rack closet into a floor-to-ceiling closet that houses all our clothes, bags, and shoes. It's become the envy of our neighborhood and one of the highlights of our new home. We installed garage closets from GarageExperts to hide all the seasonal decorative items and outdoor activity "stuff." Now everything has a place to be stored, and everything is easy to find. And the bonus is how aesthetically pleasing an organized garage is when we enter it every day.

# Chapter 3

# CHOOSE COLORS THAT INSPIRE AND ENRICH YOUR SOUL

Completing a painting project provides the maximum impact for a minimal cost and, simply, it's the most cost-effective way to achieve the transformation of a space. The cost of a gallon of paint is a lot less than purchasing new furniture or flooring. The width and height of any room's walls are large visuals that, when painted, have an instant impact on how the room is seen and how it feels.

Most of us have selected paint colors and painted the walls and ceiling of a room, and when finished, we are excited by the instant gratification of the room's transformation. Yet the challenge is when you must select paint colors for several rooms or the entire house, as all the paint color choices can be overwhelming. Many of us have experienced being in a house where every room is painted in bold, bright colors, which create a choppy or a start-and-stop feel for the entire house. Most likely, there wasn't a plan laid out for the paint colors for the entire home. It's important to take the time up front to create an entire paint color palette so you have balanced colors that complement one another and result in a good color flow from room to room.

## A Color Foundation to Build Upon

When building a new house, you need to have a strong foundation to build upon. This is the same concept to remind yourself when you are in the process of creating your paint color palette. Similarly, wouldn't you want to know what your makeup foundation color is before selecting a lipstick color? Wouldn't you want to know your suit color before you select a tie? By determining a paint color palette for your entire home up front, you will have a color foundation to work from when you must decide on other project materials such as flooring or cabinetry, tile, furniture, or fabric colors. Whether you are painting just one or two rooms now, the creation of your paint color palette for your entire house will be your roadmap today and for future painting projects. Take the time now to create a paint color palette initially for your entire house so you can build upon it for all future material decisions you will have to make.

Oftentimes, with new construction houses, all the walls and ceilings are the same boring beige color because it's an inexpensive and fast way for builders to build and sell houses. Yet once the house is sold, it's time to have it express your personality. I have experienced this with not only new construction houses but also with clients who have lived in the same house for years without ever changing one paint color from the previous homeowner. Why would you want to live in a house that doesn't represent you?

With all the homes I've lived in, and there have been many over the years, the first thing I do is create a new color paint palette for the entire house and then paint everything. I encourage you to do the same, and the result is a well-balanced color foundation that you can build upon for decades to come and a home that is representative of you. Years later, I still reference my paint color palette samples when I'm shopping for fabrics or decorative pieces. Whether you are moving into a newly constructed or previously owned house, create a new paint color palette early on so that your new colors represent you, and you will have a strong foundation of color to work with for all your future decisions.

Now that you have a clear picture of your project and budget outlined, it's time to create your paint color palette. Before you jump into painting fan decks with hundreds of shades of white, it's important to consider how color affects your mood and the properties and characteristics of color.

## How Color Affects Your Mood

Personal preferences and color schemes outlining furniture and art can all play a role in your paint color selection. Yet nothing more powerful is how a color can have a definite impact on your mood or behavior. Many studies are available online that discuss how color affects mood. Some colors make you feel energetic, while others can be calming. The type of emotional trigger is caused by the color's saturation and brightness level. I shared with you my client's Pepto-Bismol dining room and how the bright overbearing pink wall color distracted me from seeing the baby grand piano!

A good starting place to understand how paint color affects your mood is knowing that paint color falls into two groups: warm and cool. Warm colors are associated with sunlight and heat and create a lively, energetic feel to a space. Red, yellow, and orange are warm colors. Cool colors are associated with nature like water, sky, and plants. Blue, greens, and violet or purple are cool colors. Of course, there are hundreds of variations of these colors, as well as extreme colors like white and black. Let's look at how each color affects your moods and emotions.

*Red* creates excitement, stimulates conversation, and is a great choice for entries, living rooms, dining rooms, offices, and entertainment spaces. Because red is a stimulant and can often increase one's blood pressure, it is not a good choice for a bedroom or other rooms where calm and peace are the priorities.

*Yellow* is associated with warm sunshine and happiness, like a sunny summer day. Soft, lighter tones of yellow can make a space feel cheery and uplifting, yet bold, brighter tones of yellow can convey frustration or anger. Kitchens, dining rooms, and bathrooms are good rooms for a pale, soft yellow color. Be cautious when using a darker shade of yellow for a baby's nursery because of the negative emotions it can convey.

*Orange* is a combination of mixing red and yellow and has the traits of both colors. Orange creates energy and enthusiasm like red and creates a warm and inviting feeling like yellow. It's good not only for the rooms listed above but also for gyms or workout rooms.

*Blue* evokes a feeling of peace and tranquility and is shown to reduce your heart rate and lower your blood pressure. I love working with blue paint colors in bedrooms, bathrooms, and offices. Be careful though with darker blues, as they create a feeling of sadness or depression.

*Green* is a combination of mixing yellow and blue, it generates the cheeriness of yellow and the peace and tranquility of blue. It is a color abundant in nature and associated with renewal and growth. Green is my favorite color and a great choice for entries, bedrooms, kitchens, powder rooms, and dining rooms. Use caution using a mid to darker shade of green in a bathroom, as it sometimes negatively affects the lighting when applying makeup.

*Purple* is a combination of blue and red, each a cool and warm color, respectively, and the emotion it generates depends on the shade. A lighter shade of purple, like lavender, will create a tranquil emotion, whereas a darker shade, like red, will work and create energy in a room, so use them when you want to create conversation and activity. Purple is often associated with royalty and provides a luxurious feel to a space.

*White* is often associated with purity, simplicity, and cleanliness and evokes moods of quietness and concentration. I recommend choosing an off-white, which has some yellow in it to minimize any negative emotion in any room. Yet when an entire room is painted white, it can create feelings of anxiety.

*Black* absorbs all light and is the absence of color, so it's not a color at all, and that is why it is not on the color wheel. It can create a dark, depressing mood if used in an entire room. Yet painting an accent wall or trim can add sophistication and elegance to a living or dining room.

*Gray* is a combination of black and white, and it's been the new "beige" for many years now. Gray is a dull, moody, and sad color that affects the mind and body by causing unsettling feelings. It also evokes feelings of loneliness and isolation. Be careful not to paint your entire house gray and use it sparingly. A gray taupe color has gained popularity over the past few years as it is a midtone gray combined with the warmth of underlining brown tones.

## Color Properties and Characteristics

A cohesive paint color palette is created with similar color properties that balance with other elements, such as the flooring color, that will enhance the overall flow from room to room and be aesthetically pleasing. It's important to have a basic understanding of color terminology, the color wheel, color characteristics, and paint colorants before you jump into creating your paint color palette.

You may have used terms such as *hue, tint, tone*, and *shade* to describe a color, and each describes an individual color-mixing process and is important in understanding the differences between colors.

- *Hue* is the pure range of color that we can see on a color wheel. When I say "red," "blue," and "green," I'm talking about hue.
- *Tint* is created when white is added to any hue on a color wheel. The process lightens the color. Pastel colors are often tinted colors.
- *Tone* is created when gray is added to a color. The final color depends on the amount of black and white used, and the tone will be lighter or darker than the original hue which often makes the intensity of the color dull.
- *Shade* is created when black is added to a hue found on the color wheel. The process darkens the hue.

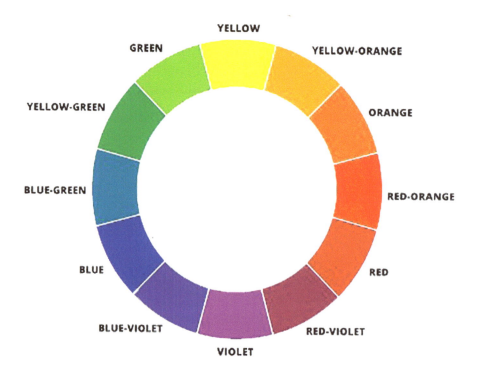

    The color wheel shows twelve colors around a circle and is used to represent each color's relationship to one another. The color wheel is an essential tool in understanding the foundational visual art principle known as color theory and consists of primary, secondary, and tertiary colors.

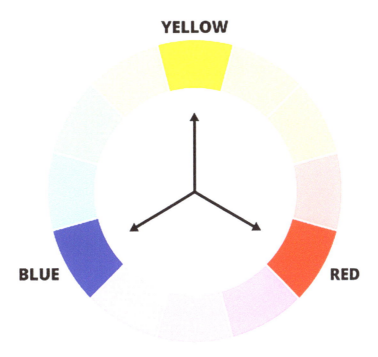

The primary colors are red, yellow, and blue, and they are the cornerstone of color as you can't mix any colors together to get these colors. When combined, they make up secondary and tertiary colors, along with all the hues in between. This powerful triad shapes the foundation of color theory as we know it. Use primary colors when you want to create a bright and cheerful space.

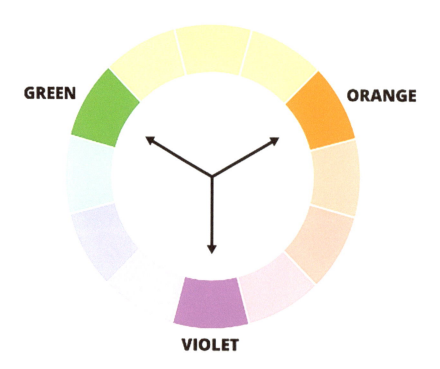

Secondary colors are the equal mixture of two primary colors, which are orange, green, and purple. Yellow and blue mix to create green, yellow and red mix to create orange, and blue and red mix to create violet. To evoke a more peaceful or relaxed feeling in a space, I recommend using secondary colors.

## TERTIARY COLORS

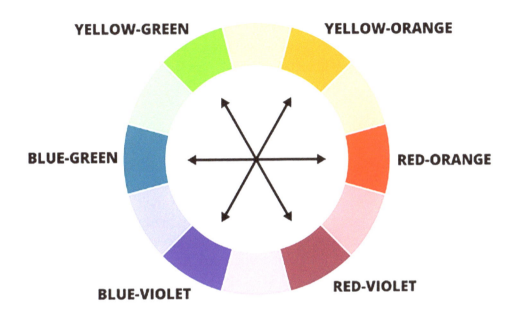

    Tertiary colors are a mixture of one primary and one secondary color next to each other on the color wheel. The six tertiary colors are yellow-orange, red-orange, red-violet, blue-violet, blue-green, and yellow-green. The colors are named from the two colors that comprise them. For example, a primary color, such as yellow, and a secondary color, such as green, mix to create yellow-green. If you want a sophisticated feel to your space, consider using tertiary colors.

    Value, also called lightness, refers to how light or dark a color is. Lighter colors have higher values. For example, orange has a higher value than navy blue or dark purple. Black has the lowest value of any hue, and white has the highest value.

    Chroma is sometimes called saturation and refers to the intensity of a color. A color with high chroma has no black, white, or gray added to it and can be considered a bright color. Highly saturated colors are vivid; low-saturated colors appear more washed out or dull.

    When it comes to making a certain paint color, paint colorants are used. A colorant is a concentrated dispersion of color pigment that is used to tint a white base paint. Most manufacturers use eight primary colors—white, cyan, magenta, yellow, red, green, blue, and black, and a maximum of four of those colors would be needed to achieve a particular color. Any one paint color recipe is made by mixing three to four different colorants. When I mixed gallons of paint for customers in my paint store, the process trained my eye as to which colorants were needed to make a specific color. The more clearly and consistently you can describe each element of color, the better you will become at seeing color undertones and detecting the subtle differences between colors. It is important that you can recognize and describe colors that will create successful combinations for any design.

Now that you have a basic understanding of the color wheel and color terms, let's explore some color schemes that will be helpful when creating your own paint color palette.

## Color Schemes

A color scheme is a combination of colors that work well together and the framework of how colors are chosen and put together. A color palette, which I've referred to a lot thus far, refers to the actual colors you've chosen based on your color scheme. By pairing different colors with each other, you can create endless color palettes to use in any composition. Different color combinations evoke different moods and see what color scheme and feeling you are attracted to before you start flipping through fan decks. These color schemes will outline which colors you gravitate toward that align with the look and feel of your project.

*Monochromatic schemes*

A monochromatic color scheme is comprised of variations of one color. The dominant color forms the base of the scheme, and all other colors are derivatives of that color. You can use any color to create a monochromatic color scheme. For example, adding white to red creates pink, and adding black to red creates maroon. Then you can have a monochromatic color scheme of pink, red, and maroon.

Start by selecting a base color, which will be the dominant color for your walls and décor plan. Next, select at least two options off the base color—one lighter and one darker. A paint manufacturer fan deck is a good place to start to see the color variations, and it's important to make sure the colors are different enough to provide a contrast. This color scheme is perfect for creating a calm and serene feel and is often used to make a space feel larger. It is very versatile and easy on the eye.

*Complementary schemes*

    Complementary schemes are composed by using two colors opposite each other on the color wheel. This scheme will naturally include a warm and a cool color, as they're on opposite sides of the wheel. The main color is considered dominant, while the complement serves as an accent. The three traditional combinations are red and green, yellow and purple, and orange and blue. The complementary colors will contain a warm and cool color and create high contrast when used together and play up each other's intensity while appearing balanced since they equally stimulate different parts of the eye.

*Analogous schemes*

    Analogous schemes are colors that are next to each other on the color wheel and typically comprised three colors. A scheme of blue-green, green, and green-yellow is an example of an analogous color scheme. Start by selecting one dominant color; the second and third colors can function as the main supportive and accent colors. The colors will have enough visual interest to create contrast but still feel cohesive and complete. The scheme can be harmonious and relaxing.

*Triad scheme*

    Triad color schemes are created with three colors that are evenly spaced around the color wheel to form an equilateral triangle. This is another scheme that benefits from selecting one dominant color and two accent colors. A scheme of green, purple, and orange is an example of a triad color scheme. Depending on the saturation of each color, they can often create a vibrant and playful feel.

*Split complementary*

 The split complementary color scheme uses three colors and is created by selecting one color from the color wheel and then using one color from either side of its complementary color. It's a variation of the complementary color scheme and mixes three colors instead of two. A scheme of orange, green, and red is an example of a split complementary color scheme. This color scheme is a strong contrast of colors and can be more pleasing than a standard complementary setup but also has a chance of feeling chaotic or cluttered.

*Tetradic color scheme*

Tetradic color schemes are two sets of complementary pairs of colors that are found opposite each other on the color wheel and a form rectangle on the color wheel. It is an aggressive scheme made of variations of red, orange, yellow, and green colors that are used with one dominant color and three accent colors to create a harmonized tetradic color scheme. This is the most challenging of color schemes to pull off, yet if done effectively, it can result in a one-of-a-kind effect. The scheme is always vibrant, as there is equal tension between all colors. Combine warm and cool tones for a dramatic feel or muted tones for a pleasant feel.

Once you've gravitated to a particular color scheme, there are a few more important elements that need to be considered before starting to create your paint color palette.

## Natural Light

The position of a house on a lot and the number and size of all the windows all play a role in how the natural light affects all the walls, ceiling, doors, and trim paint colors. When creating a paint color palette for a client, I prefer to work during the midday hours as the natural light will have the most impact on how the paint colors are experienced in each room. I've partnered with several clients who live by the ocean or a lake, and the glare off the water during daylight hours has a definite effect on the interior paint colors and is something to keep in mind if you live by the water.

For one of my clients it took several selections over a few days to get the right paint color finalized as the glare from the ocean had such an impact on how the colors were seen on the interior walls.

## Flooring Colors

Flooring is an expensive budget item and doesn't change unless you are doing extensive remodeling. All flooring materials have color variations to them, and whether it's existing or new flooring, they need to be considered when selecting paint colors. Place your paint color samples on the hardwood or tile floor to get a better perspective on each underlying color. If you are building a house, I recommend working with flooring samples—the larger, the better—and paint color samples in the house when possible.

Working in a flooring showroom to select paint colors is not recommended as oftentimes a showroom will have fluorescent lighting that is not conducive to your house and, in turn, will influence the flooring and paint color samples. Work with flooring and paint color samples in your house so you can experience the natural light and how it affects you both throughout the day and at night. It's important to understand the underlying colors of your floor material so that it balances with your new paint color palette.

## Room Flow

If you are painting several rooms that connect through a hallway or into an open space, decide the location of each color, and determine where the color starts and where it stops. It's easy if all your rooms are in square boxes, but oftentimes, you want to change to a different paint color where there are curved walls or rooms with angled ceilings. A good guideline to use is that all horizontal spaces are the wall color, and all the vertical spaces are the ceiling color. It's best to start and stop a paint color in a corner or edge of a wall. There are exceptions to every rule, and this is a good guideline to start with.

## Ceilings, Doors, and Trim

Think of your room as a box, and the ceiling is the top of the box and is your fifth wall. The horizontal alignment of the ceiling not only affects how the wall color will be impacted but also how a space will feel. Balance the top of the box or ceiling paint color with your flooring color, or bottom of the box, to create a balanced look.

Most clients gravitate to a "white" ceiling yet oftentimes don't take into consideration the flooring color, which is also an important element to achieve a balance between the ceiling and floor colors. There are many versions of white, and you can see this the minute you open a fan deck of paint colors by any paint manufacturer. Some undertones make up a cool white or warm white, and once you understand the difference, you can find the right white color that balances the wall paint color and flooring color. Additionally, there are other options than a white ceiling to explore, and the key is to consider all the other elements in the space to find the right ceiling color. Perhaps explore a soft blue or green in a tone that balances with your wall paint color to create a truly unique space.

The interior doors and all the trim for the windows, doors, and baseboards all play roles when creating your paint color palette. Most clients gravitate to the standard white paint color for their doors and all the trim so to offset these elements from the paint wall color. But if your room or house has a lot of trim work and you want to minimize all of it, then consider painting the doors and trim a different color other than white. The painting of doors and trim in the same paint color as the walls will enhance the room flow and make the spaces feel larger. The important thing is to select a paint color for the ceiling, doors, and trim that are of similar undertones to the wall paint color and are well-balanced. The same door and trim color must be used throughout the entire house to achieve continuity and an aesthetic pleasing look.

The repainting or restaining of existing trim and doors must be considered when deciding both on your new paint color palette and on your painting project budget. The painting of existing trim and doors can add up to half the total cost of the entire paint project, as it is often labor-intensive. Some professional painters use sprayers for this type of work, while others remove all the trim and doors and paint them off-site. Both have varying timelines to complete, which may impact your budget. Discuss the labor costs and timelines with your paint contractor before the project begins. If you can afford to paint or restain the trim and doors throughout your entire house, I highly recommend doing it, as you may regret it later once you have newly painted walls and ceilings.

## Paint Samples and Finishes

Once you've narrowed down your choices to two to three paint colors per room, you are now ready to get your hands dirty with paint. Purchase small containers, if possible, or a quart and apply two coats of paint on at least a three-by-three-foot-square space on two different walls in the room, as the light will affect how the colors look on each wall. If you are nervous about applying color to your walls, then purchase large pieces of heavy stock paper at your local craft store and apply two coats of paint on them, and once dry, tape them on the walls.

Another option is to use color samples with adhesive backing, like Sherwin-Williams' eight-by-eight-inch samples of their most popular colors. Purchase multiple samples of the same color and place them on different walls in the same room. Review the paint colors for several days both during the day and at night, as other elements such as natural light, water reflection, tinted windows, or interior lighting can affect how they will be experienced. Sample all your paint colors prior to committing to purchasing all the paint for your project.

All paint manufacturers have different types of finish options available with their interior and exterior paint lines, and I recommend partnering with your local paint store staff to assist you with selecting the right finish. A good guideline is to apply an eggshell or satin finish for the walls, a flat finish for the ceilings, and a semi-gloss for the trim and doors. Depending on the paint manufacturer, some flat paints nowadays are durable for wall applications and provide a matte look, which is a current trend.

Most professional painters stick with a particular brand of paint they like best for all types of applications, and some brands are more expensive than others. Rely on your painter's expertise when it comes to selecting the paint brand to use. If you've ventured into painting yourself, stick with a brand you like that works within your budget. Like most things, technology is constantly improving the quality of paint products and your painter or staff at your local paint store can guide you on the best available finishes for your application needs.

Make sure to write down all your final paint colors, including finishes, locations of each paint color, and any new recipe numbers if a color change was made. Keep all color samples of your final color palette in your project folder or bin in one place for future reference. I assure you that you will want to reference this list for future touchups or color changes that you may want to make in the years to come.

## Color Consultants

While guiding clients in the creation of their paint color palettes for decades, I've witnessed all kinds of emotions and scenarios throughout the process. Committing to change your house paint colors can be scary and overwhelming for many, and emotions range from tears to sheer panic to heated arguments between couples or the anxious painter that needs all the paint colors finalized yesterday so the project can start. The tools I've outlined here for you are designed to help you create a paint color palette you love and to minimize the stress and negative emotions that can be attributed to making paint color decisions.

If you find yourself stuck and emotional when making paint color decisions, consider partnering with a color consultant who can create a new paint color palette that you love for now and for all future remodeling projects. A color consultant will experience the interior of your house and take into consideration the important elements, such as the natural light, the room layout, and the flooring material, to ensure the final color palette will be cohesive and aesthetically pleasing. They will also understand all the important elements to consider when selecting exterior paint colors.

Many color consultants I've met are interior or graphic designers and understand the properties, characteristics, and all the important elements to consider when selecting paint colors. My knowledge was enhanced by mixing paint in my paint store, which provided me with a firsthand understanding of how combining paint colorants creates a specific color. You can search for local color consultants or inquire with your local paint store for referrals. Their expertise is invaluable and an investment in building your color foundation for years to come.

# CHAPTER 4

# TRANSFORMING ELEMENTS

Interior Furnishings

A house is the physical structure of a place to live, and a home is an expression of the occupants of the house. As I mentioned earlier in my introduction, the word *home* resonates with being relaxed and comfortable, in harmony with one's surroundings. The following elements will be a guide to transforming your physical house into a home that you love and are proud to share with friends and family for generations to come.

You now have your paint color palette finalized, and it's time to turn your focus to the furnishings for either a specific room or your entire home. And now you can understand the importance of your paint color palette, which creates the foundation for all current and future material choices that lie ahead. When venturing into the world of furniture shopping without an interior designer, I recommend you have your new color palette paint samples with you when shopping at your local retail furniture stores. The samples will help you stay on your new color path when you're researching and finalizing all the furniture upholstery fabrics and finishes.

*Room zones*

Nowadays, many homes have an open floor plan, and there are many zones in any house. Examples include a drop zone, a conversation zone, an entertainment zone, or a work zone. I consider a drop zone to be any place where you "drop" keys, cell phones, bookbags, or groceries. Do you have a mudroom or an entry console table that becomes a drop zone? It's best to have a conversation area away from a doorway, and oftentimes, they are centered around a fireplace or room focal point. Determine the optimal seating requirements for the conversation zone, and then decide which existing furniture pieces you want to keep and which pieces you want or need to purchase. A sofa or sectional, a sitting chair or chairs, and coffee and end tables are good pieces to have for a balanced conversation zone. Other zones to consider are entertainment zones that may include a wet bar or game table, coffee zones that include all coffee-related items in one area, or office or work zones that include a workspace for a laptop and phone chargers. Some or all can be incorporated into open floor plans, depending on the size of your living space.

*Kitchen and bathrooms*

Your kitchen and bathroom are designated zones within a house, and the physical layout of the appliances and plumbing fixtures are set unless you are doing extensive remodeling or constructing a new house. If you are planning to remodel or build new, I recommend partnering with an interior designer who will design the space and choose materials for optimal functionality.

A good guideline for kitchens is to use the tried-and-true triangle alignment of the cooktop, or range, the sink, and the refrigerator for easy access while working in the space. It's best to have approximately four feet of clearance between an island and the work surrounding, which provides enough space for multiple people to be cooking and moving about. Consider other zones when designing a new kitchen, including a cooking zone, such as a cooktop and ovens; the cleaning zone, such as the sink or sinks; the consumable zone, such as your refrigerator or pantry; the nonconsumable zone, such as where your pots and pans are stored; and the prep zone, which is the area you do all the food prep in.

If you have the space in your new kitchen, a double island is pure luxury and can provide extra prep and storage space. Bring in your personality through artwork, photographs, antiques, or other decorative items that are in balance with the room and pleasing to view.

The bathroom layout of the plumbing fixtures is determined by the size of the room and the location of the actual plumbing in the space. Oftentimes, the layout of the vanity, tub, shower, and toilet is set, so consider changing the paint color on the walls or on the vanity for a new look or incorporating art on the walls and, if space allows, decorative accessories on shelving. If you are remodeling your bathroom, align your tile selections with your color palette and choose larger tiles if you want minimal grout lines and to make a smaller space feel larger.

*Furniture layouts*

For your rooms with furniture, take measurements of the room or rooms, including all the windows, doors, hallways, and any accent features like a fireplace. Then measure the width, depth, and height of all the existing furniture pieces you want to use in the space. Measure twice and purchase once is a good guideline. Incorporate all the measurements into a furniture layout tool like Room Sketcher, or draw out the measurements on grid paper. There are a lot of great layout tools online, so do some research, and download what works for your skill set. Once you have a drawing of your existing furniture pieces, you can then draw in the approximate size of the new furniture pieces you want to purchase. Most drawing tools have images of individual furniture pieces that you can drag and drop into your layout, and some incorporate specifics from national furniture suppliers. Furniture that is the wrong size will stick out and create an imbalance for the entire room.

Another important consideration when laying out furniture is determining the traffic flow. Especially with open floor plans, it's critical that you have flow between the living zone and the dining or entertainment zone and place furniture within each zone.

Living room furniture layout

The ideal seating arrangement encourages intimate conversation while offering enough walking space. To achieve a balanced furniture layout, decide if there is a focal point in the room. Often a fireplace or view, such as the ocean or a beautiful landscape, is the focal point, and the arrangement of furniture needs to highlight it in a balanced way.

If a fireplace is the focal point of the room, determine an anchor furniture piece, such as a sofa or sectional, and center it in front of it. Or if you have a larger room, you can place two sofas or one sofa and two sitting chairs on either side of the fireplace. If you have a beautiful ocean or landscape view as your focal point, consider working with swivel chairs or a bench in front of the view, along with a sofa, and other furniture pieces to create your conversation zone. A coffee table is placed in front of the sofa or sectional, and end tables are placed on either end of the sofa or one at one end if space is an issue. A small drink table can be placed in between the two sitting chairs for easy access.

A TV oftentimes is the focal point of a family room, and whether it's above or next to a fireplace, you want to center your sofa or sectional in front of it and the correct distance from it for the most comfortable viewing for everyone. Avoid having a walkway in front of a TV as it can be distracting for viewing.

Distance guidelines for living room furniture

- Fourteen- to eighteen-inch distance from coffee table or end table to seating pieces
- Thirty- to thirty-six-inch distance between furniture seating pieces
- Eight to ten feet is the maximum space you want to leave between seating.
- One and a half or two times the size of the TV is the distance from the TV to the center of your sofa or sectional.
- Seven- to eight-inch clearance between the top of a mantel and the base of a flat-screen TV, twenty-inch minimum distance between a fireplace and TV, and sixty- to eighty-inch maximum height from the floor to the TV.

Dining room furniture layout

Have you sat at a dining room table and didn't have enough room to comfortably get in and out of the dining chair? This is an example of the furniture pieces being too large for the dining space and can have an impact on how the room feels when entertaining. It's best to center your dining table and chair in the room or zone and position another piece such as a sideboard or buffet on a large wall near the table. You want to have enough space to walk around the table and behind chairs and to use other pieces to open a drawer or cabinet doors.

Distance guidelines for dining room furniture

- Thirty- to thirty-six-inch distance between the table and other furniture pieces. This allows for enough room for guests to walk behind chairs while others are seated or to open a drawer or cabinet when you need to get an item out.
- Twenty-four-inch distance from the dining table to the edge of the area rug. This is the minimum space that will accommodate chairs to sit on an area rug when pulled away from the table.
- Twenty-four-inch distance between dining room chairs. This provides elbow room and ample space to get in and out of the chair comfortably.

Bedroom furniture layout

Bedroom furniture placement consists of a bed, two nightstands, a dresser, and, depending on the room size, a sitting chair or bench that can be incorporated into the space. Center the bed on the largest wall, and place nightstands on either side of it. If your bed will only fit on a window wall, add a window covering, such as drapery, to act as a headboard.

Additionally, if you don't have a headboard, you can use multiple-sized euro pillows to act as one. A solid headboard that is securely attached to your bed is a good feng shui principle to follow when you are laying out your bedroom furniture. A strong headboard adds a sense of security to the room.

Place a dresser on a wall that is in proportion to its size if possible. And remember, do not have a TV in the bedroom; it must be a peaceful room to rest in and not be distracted by the visuals and sounds of a television.

Distance guidelines for bedroom furniture

- Three inches from the bed to the nightstands. A minimal distance for furniture to not to look crowded and enough reach to your lamp or alarm clock.
- Twenty-four inches between the bed and the wall or dresser. A minimal distance for walking around the bed for opening and closing drawers of your dresser or closet doors.

A furniture layout drawing is a great visual to see how your room will look once completed. Make sure to print out and bring with you the layout drawing and measurements, along with your paint color samples on your next shopping trip. You will then be armed and ready to start on your furniture adventure.

When I've partnered with clients for new furniture purchases, I always discuss which pieces will be investment pieces—the pieces you want to have for a long time in your home. Ask yourself which piece of furniture you want to invest in that is of better quality and will endure life's changes. When we were deciding on our new living room sectional, I educated Rick on the quality of workmanship of the manufacturer and discussed the specifics of the sectional's internal components and the durability of the upholstery fabric before we discussed the price. After some resistance about the cost, he decided that a sectional would be the investment piece that we will have for a long time. He shares this story with colleagues, friends, and family to this day.

An interior designer can guide you toward finding the right investment piece for your home. A designer is knowledgeable about the furniture manufacturer's customization process, like changing the seat depth or height on a sofa or creating a custom finish for a dining room table. Additionally, they have access to thousands of upholstery fabrics to choose from. Customizing a new piece of furniture may be more expensive than purchasing it at retail, yet it is worth the investment as the result will be a piece that is truly unique, of superior quality, and will outlast a piece purchased on sale from a discount furniture store.

*Area rugs*

One consistent flooring material throughout the main floor of a house is very popular nowadays, and most often, the floor material of choice is engineered hardwood or luxury vinyl material. An area rug is critical to defining each zone, and it grounds the energy in the space. Area rugs improve the acoustics of space by absorbing sound and are particularly important in a room that has predominantly hard surfaces, in which sound bounces off and creates an echo that can hinder conversation.

Once you have the right-size furniture and layout of each piece, you can determine the correct size area rug you need by drawing a rug on your furniture layout. A guideline is to have eight to twelve inches of bare floor around it in a small room and twenty to twenty-four inches of bare floor around it in a large room. Area rugs come in various standard sizes, such as eight-by-ten feet or nine-by-twelve feet, yet sometimes these sizes don't work for your space, and you need to consider a custom-size rug. The last thing you want to do is purchase a new area rug in the wrong size and have the furniture hanging off the sides. I see this mistake often, and it can make a room feel unbalanced and out of scale if the furniture is not properly placed on an area rug. Research many online and retail stores that offer custom sizes for area rugs. In chapter, 5 I will share with you an easy and cost-effective way to make custom area rugs.

*Reupholster and refinish*

I'm often asked if reupholstering or refinishing furniture pieces is worth the money, and I always inquire as to the sentimental attachment and discuss the size and location of the piece. Depending on the cost of the upholstery fabric, the reupholstery labor costs are typically the same or often higher than purchasing a new chair. Yet if the chair has sentimental value attached to it and fits in the space, then reupholstering it can bring it back to life and become your favorite new piece of furniture. Sometimes the furniture piece is not suitable for a particular room in the home and should be donated.

A client several years ago received several antique pieces from a family member, and all had varying degrees of damage to them. Each piece has sentimental value to her, and we partnered with a local furniture refinisher to restore all of them for her. After many months with the refinisher, they all turned out beautifully and are now treasures in her home. Determine the location and size of the furniture piece that needs reupholstering or refinishing before deciding on moving ahead with the project.

Decide early in the process as to which pieces of furniture you currently have or need to purchase and which pieces you have wanted to have for a long time. If you are purchasing a new sectional sofa, invest in a good-quality piece and durable upholstery fabric. If you've decided that you love your older sofa and want to reupholster it in a new durable upholstery fabric, then consider this your investment piece. This applies similarly to any furniture items that you want to refinish.

*Decorative accessories*

Decorative accessories are an important finishing touch to a room and not only add interest but also reveal some of your personality. National retailers, like Home Goods, At Home, or Pottery Barn; online home décor manufacturers; or your local home décor retailers offer an abundance of accessory choices to add spice and finish any room. Coffee table books, vases, bowls, faux greenery, sculptures, artifacts, and candles all come in various colors, shapes, and sizes and are just some types of accessories I like to work with. The colors of each piece will play back to your paint color palette, which you already have in hand while you're out shopping. Vary the textures, shapes, sizes, and placement of each piece. A good guideline is to decorate in threes for optimum balance. Odd-number groupings, such as five, seven, and nine, also work to create a memorable, appealing look more so than even-number groupings. For example, the placement of three large-size coffee table books stacked on the table along with a medium-sized faux plant placed off to one side and a small artifact on top of the books will create interest and tell a well-balanced story versus the placement of one candle on the coffee table.

A less-is-more approach to decorating with accessories is a good guideline to use. When you have finished decorating your living room, stand back and experience your work. Often, it's best to edit some pieces and use them later. Become a guest in your own room, and try to see what others see and feel.

*Balance*

Balance is an important element to regularly check when deciding on your room's furnishings. Stand back from your furniture arrangement, and see if all the elements are in balance with one another. Are the fabric colors and textures in balance with the style of the furniture? Are the finishes of the coffee table, end tables, and console tables similar and complemented the fabrics and paint color palette? Is the area rug's design and color in balance with the furniture and fabrics? These are all good questions to answer when deciding if your furniture is balanced in your space.

If your space has a lot of hard edges, angles, or other room elements, consider incorporating items with soft edges or curves to them to provide softness and good energy flow. A sitting chair with sloped arms, a round coffee table, or curved glass pendant lights are some ways to bring balance and softness to other pieces or elements that have hard-edged details.

*Easy changes for positive energy flow*

As you personally change and grow, so should your home. Hopefully, your style and tastes change over time, and these changes should be reflected throughout your home environment. Movement within your home keeps the energy flowing, and that's a positive way to live. I find that making seasonal changes with decorative pieces is an easy and inexpensive way to check in with myself and my home's energy. Some inexpensive ways to renew your home's interiors include the following:

- Rearrange furniture pieces in a room to a new location. Is a living room sitting chair calling to be in the master bedroom?
- Reupholster worn-out dining chair cushions. Add a new color or pattern to your cushions, and most projects can be a DIY with a new fabric and stapler.
- Rearrange or purchase new decorative pillows in a new color and fabric. Discount home décor stores make this a simple and easy way to freshen any room. Try various fabric textures, shapes, and sizes for added interest.
- Rearrange pictures or paintings on a wall or shelf. Simple movements of artwork throughout your home are easy ways to bring new life to a different space.

- Reframe photographs in similar styles and color frames. Similar picture frame finishes are aesthetically pleasing to the eye and provide continuity.
- Rearrange accessories such as vases, candles, and faux greens into bedrooms, offices, laundry, flex room, and living room for a fresh new look.
- Replace old ceiling mount light fixtures with a new fixture in a new finish and one that requires LED bulbs for better lighting.
- Replace dated cabinet hardware with simple, clean-lined pulls and/or knobs in polished nickel or antique brass finish. Don't forget your front door hardware as a new one will bring a fresh new look to your important front entrance!

## Window Coverings

While growing up in New England, draperies were often used as window coverings because of the traditional style that complemented the traditional architecture of most houses. They add beautiful drama to a room while helping to contain heat during the winter months and protecting against the heat in the space during the summer months. Yet when I relocated to the west coast, living without any window coverings was more common as the views and natural light, especially during Seattle winters, drove decisions to keep windows uncovered. This concept was foreign to me, as I looked at window coverings as a finishing detail and an integral part of any interior design project. Draperies, Roman shades, and any other style of window covering are important details not to overlook when finishing a room.

## The Finishing Touch

If you've never had or are unsure about having window coverings in your home, I recommend that you stand back and view your room during the evening hours. Depending on the number and size of your room's windows, you will see a lot of black seeping through all the windows and into your warm and cozy room. How does all the blackness coming into your room make you feel? Does the blackness balance with your interior's color palette and furnishings?

The night's blackness can oftentimes overpower a room or entire home if not covered. Wouldn't you want to have window coverings that are closed when you are entertaining friends in your living room on a cold winter's evening? Consider how your space feels without window coverings, and then consider how it might feel with window coverings. Whether it's a simple roller shade that can hide behind a valance or draperies that can add texture and drama to your dining room windows, a window covering changes how your room looks and feels and is an important element to making a room look and feel finished.

Window coverings also provide privacy, and we all want privacy in our homes, especially if your neighbor can see right through your kitchen or bedroom window. Window coverings can protect hardwood floors and furniture pieces from sunlight that can cause discoloration or damage. We all want to have beautiful natural light pouring into our rooms, which we can still achieve with the right window covering for our situation. Sunshades are a great solution if you need to manage the amount of light you want in and still see out when the shades are down.

Remodeling or building a house is an undertaking, for sure, and very often, window coverings are not considered or budgeted for until the very end of the project. I understand that there are a lot of material decisions that need to be finalized to complete a remodel or build a new house. Yet the last thing you want to do after a long remodel or new build is realized that you don't have any window coverings, and you end up nailing sheets to the walls for privacy. Create a window covering line items in your budget upfront, and plan instead of scrambling at the end.

## Styles

Window covering manufacturers revise their textures and colors regularly to stay on the current trend. Hunter Douglas and Horizons are just some of the manufacturers that I partner with as they offer a great variety of window-covering solutions. And other national retailers, like The Shade Store, have a good selection of window covering options to fit your budget and needs. Some window covering styles to consider include the following:

*Drapery*

If you desire custom draperies or fabric Roman shades, I encourage you to partner with an interior designer, as they can guide you with the fabric and hardware selections and oversee the workroom and installation process. A drapery's purpose is to block light, provide privacy, and add visual interest to the space. They provide moderate blackout light blocking, depending on the fabric and lining material. The drapery panels are installed on the outside of the window frame and casing and hang on a rod with rings, hooks, or grommets. The top treatments come in various pleat styles and other styles, including ripplefold, rod pocket, tab top, or grommet.

*Shades*

Shades come in various types of fabric and other materials, such as woven weaves or vinyl. To let in light and see outside, you need to raise the shade using either a cord, roller, or lifting mechanism. They are attached to the inside of the window frame and provide moderate blackout light blocking. Roman, roller, woven wood, cellular, or pleated shades are some examples to explore.

*Blinds*

Blinds are composed of slats, also called louvers, that tilt open to let in light or close for darkness and privacy. And unlike shades, you don't have to fully raise blinds to see through them; you can just tilt them open. They provide moderate to high light blocking. Wood, vertical, or metal blinds are some examples to explore.

## Layering and Motorization

Once you understand the importance of window coverings, yet budget is a concern, consider covering a window with a Roman or roller shade that is installed on the inside of the window trim. Later, when your budget allows, you can add a layer such as a drapery panel or a valance on the outside of the window for added coverage and functionality. Layering different window covering styles customizes your windows, and their fabrics and textures provide interest, color, and warmth to the glass area of the window.

Today, all window covering manufacturers have motorization options, and they are a great, easy solution for spaces, especially in rooms with tall windows. Our new living room windows are over six feet tall, and I installed motorized roller sunshades. With the click of a button, we control the sunlight coming in and the privacy. Technological advancements allow you to control your motorized shades through an app on your phone or through Siri, and they are very popular. Imagine being at work on a hot summer day and forgetting to close all your shades before leaving the house. From an app on your phone, you can close all of them from your office or car and arrive at a nice, cool home. Like my analogy with moving away from wire rack closet systems to custom built-in closets, once you have motorized window coverings in your home or office, it's hard to go back to manual systems.

When you are deciding on window coverings for your home, it's important to see how each will look from the outside of your home before you place an order. For a consistent and pleasing look, choose linings or weaves in the same color, especially for windows facing the front of your house. Imagine if each window facing the front had different window-covering colors and styles. How would this feel when you approached your home from the street? You can mix styles and colors throughout your home, but always consider the windows on the front of your home, and make sure you will see similar window covering colors in your windows when the coverings are down or closed.

## Lighting

When choosing lighting for your home, consider the different functions that each room serves before you start shopping. For example, a home office will need brighter task lighting, while a living room might benefit from more ambient lighting to create a relaxing atmosphere. By carefully considering and planning the lighting in each room, you can create the perfect atmosphere for every space in your house. If your remodeling or building project requires an extensive plan, I recommend partnering with an electrician or a local lighting designer for assistance in selecting the right type, style, output, temperature color, and quantity of lighting for your needs. A lighting plan is key to ensuring you have the right amount and type of light for your application.

Understanding the four types of lighting can help you decide the best solution for your home.

### *Types*

*Ambient* illuminates the entire room and is made for a single purpose. Examples include recessed ceiling lights, chandeliers, wall sconces, and track lights.

*Task* illuminates areas where you perform certain tasks, such as food preparation, reading, or writing. Examples include under cabinet lights, pendant lights, downward directional fixtures, table or desk lamps, tape lighting, landscape lights, and bath vanity lights.

*Accent* illuminates to highlight specific features in a room, like entrances, architectural elements, artwork, or fireplaces. Examples include wall lights such as sconces or picture lights, track lights, or landscape lights.

*Decorative* illumination is used purely for aesthetic purposes, to add an extra touch of style. Examples include candelabras, wall sconces, or string lights.

Lumens, commonly known as brightness or light output, measure how much light you are getting from a bulb. More lumens mean a brighter light; fewer lumens mean a dimmer light. An average-sized living room requires one thousand to two thousand lumens to provide an adequate amount of light. If you want to replace a one-hundred-watt bulb, look for a bulb that requires one thousand six hundred lumens. Wattage is a measure of how much electricity or energy a light bulb consumes to achieve its lumen output. Many light fixtures today display lumen requirements instead of wattage, and there are online tools to determine the correct number of lumens needed for the square footage of your space. And you can search online for the wattage equivalent if you desire.

Have you needed to purchase light bulbs recently and visited a national retailer and witnessed the number of options available to go through? The days of purchasing a seventy-five-watt incandescent bulb are slowly vanishing, and the different types of bulbs and color temperatures to consider can quickly become overwhelming. No matter what type of lighting you choose, try to make sure to use energy-efficient bulbs. LED bulbs are a great option as they last longer and use less electricity than traditional incandescent bulbs.

*Bulb color*

Color temperature describes the color shading of the light given off, and it's important to understand as the type of light will affect how your room feels. You may think that the color temperature is odd because the high temperature is described as cooler colors. It is measured in degrees of Kelvin (K) on a scale from one thousand to ten thousand. One of my clients felt best with cooler light colors, not just for her light fixtures but for her furniture finishes, fabrics, accessories, and interior paint colors. Maintain the same bulb color throughout your home, especially if you have an open floor plan, as different bulb colors in the same open space will be distracting and will create an imbalance. You can change the bulb color in a specific room yet be cognoscente of the effect the light-color difference will have on any adjacent rooms. As we've discussed, consider how you want your room to feel first, and then select the color temperature of the light source to best suit you and your environment.

*Location and size*

Consider the light fixture's location and size when deciding on the style of a fixture to purchase. A recent client purchased a house that had over twenty-five small, outdated recessed lights just in the kitchen space, and so many lights made the room feel like you were on a plane on a landing strip. To bring some calmness to the kitchen ceiling, we removed over half the number of lights and increased the size of the lights to minimize the busyness and provide a better output of light for the entire kitchen area. The larger-size light is now in balance with the size of the kitchen and is aesthetically pleasing.

I've experienced some homes where the residents only use recessed ceiling lights as their primary light source, which can be hard on the eyes when performing tasks, such as reading. The downward light from a table lamp casts a warm light ideal for tasks such as reading and creates a warm, inviting mood for the room. An end table height is anywhere from twenty-two to twenty-four inches, and a good range for a table lamp height is twenty-five to thirty-six inches. There are many styles of lamp bases and materials that are important to balance with your room's scale, color palette, and other design elements. Consider floor lamps next to or behind a sitting chair for reading or to bring light to a dark corner of a room. Table and floor lamps are not only functional types of task lighting but can also be an accent or decorative feature in a room. Combinations of task and ambient lighting are optimal solutions for most of your lighting needs.

The use of multiple pendant lights over a kitchen island has been the de facto standard for years and is a bit tiresome for me, as there are many other island lighting solutions to consider. If your kitchen and island are smaller, multiple pendants can distract from other elements in the kitchen and/or great room, so consider inexpensive recessed cans, ceiling tracks, or a single horizontal-shaped pendant instead of multiple hanging pendants. If you have a larger kitchen and island, perhaps a chandelier will provide ample task lighting and add a decorative element to your kitchen.

Wall sconces can provide the lighting you need while adding interest and dimension to an entry or accent wall and also highlighting art with their placement on either side. Consider the size of the artwork, the size of the wall sconces, and the size of the entire space to ensure the correct light output is achieved. Keep in mind the balance between the light fixture, artwork, and other furnishings such as a console table or bench. Wall sconces with adjustable arms installed above bedroom night tables are another solution to consider. Another bathroom lighting option to consider is a pendant or wall sconce instead of the standard vanity lights that are installed over a mirror.

I installed pendant lights in our new powder room and coordinated the polished nickel fixtures with a round polished nickel mirror over the vanity to complete the room. An electrician can add electrical boxes to most walls or ceilings and the addition of new wall sconces in your entry, accent wall, or bedroom will be a look for everyone to enjoy.

Lighting manufacturers continue to push the style boundaries, and online access to manufacturers' websites makes it easy to search by style, finish, lumens, wattage, and other requirements so you can find the right fixture for your space. Visual Comfort, Arteriors Home, and Hudson Valley are some of my favorite lighting manufacturers. In addition to searching manufacturer websites for your favorite light fixtures, also visit your local lighting retailers to experience the fixtures in person and the quality of the manufacturer selections. Light fixture prices and styles can range from inexpensive with minimal styling to expensive with unique styling. Determine the type of lighting and budget before you begin your research. It's time to venture out of the norm and explore new lighting solutions for your home.

## The Exterior of Your House

The outside of your house communicates a great deal about you and your family to your neighborhood and community. We've all driven by a house that needs a fresh coat of paint, has overgrown bushes that need pruning, or has bikes and sporting goods scattered all over the front yard.

*What does it say about you?*

Ask yourself, What is the exterior of my house saying about me to all my neighbors and community? I mentioned earlier about becoming a guest in your own house so you can see and feel your house, and just like the interior, the same works for the exterior of your house. Stay by the street, close your eyes, relax, and then open them. What are the first things you see? Is it toys and sports gear thrown all over the front yard and driveway, or overgrown shrubs and a dirty entrance to the front door? Energy needs a clear path to move from the street in front of your house to your front entry and a welcoming appearance so it can enter through the front door and into your home.

As I mentioned in chapter 3, the creation of a paint color palette is an important foundation to build upon for all your current and future material choices. If you need to or desire a new exterior paint color, the coloring of exterior elements such as the roof, windows, stone, or brick plays a role in deciding on all your exterior paint or stain colors. Unless you are building a new house and can select the roof, window, and stone colors prior to the build, the colors of these elements oftentimes don't change, and each plays an integral part in the exterior color palette.

The painting of your house is an expensive project, so you want to make sure you select the right colors that you will love for many years to come. If you can't get your head around selecting all the exterior paint colors and how they need to balance with all the existing materials, then I encourage you to partner with a color consultant to create a palette for you. It will be money well spent, knowing that you have a new exterior paint color palette that complements all the other elements of your house and creates a smile on your face when you drive up the driveway or walk through the front door.

Feng shui principles can also be helpful when selecting exterior paint colors, as they can guide you as to which paint or stain colors are best to use, depending on the position of your house. The chi, or energy, related to feng shui shares the importance of not only the type of front door but also its color. Doors with glass or glass side panels are not the best solution, whereas a door made of solid wood is. Selecting a front door paint color that complements or accents the body and trim paint or stain colors will communicate a lot about you and your style.

*Exterior and interior balance*

A balance in your exterior and interior paint colors and furnishings creates a positive energy flow from the outside living to the inside living for all your home's occupants and guests. Refer back to our paint color palette that you've already created to achieve an outdoor-indoor living balance. Bring similar colors from your color palette into your outdoor living spaces for a well-balanced flow, and consider outdoor furniture pieces such as sofas and sectionals, sitting chairs, coffee tables, area rugs, and light fixtures to create outdoor living rooms. Small houses may only have a front porch or small back patio, but you can still create a living room feel with the right-size furniture pieces like a sitting chair or bench that are adorned with pillows, a throw, and an area rug to anchor the pieces. Decorate both your back and front outdoor living spaces with seasonal plantings, and explore the many outdoor lighting options and decorative accessory pieces for the finishing touches to complete your new outdoor sanctuary.

*Easy ways to refresh your exterior entry*

If painting the exterior of your home is not part of your budget, then try some of these simple tips to refresh the exterior of your home.

- Front door paint: Paint or stain your front door in a new color for a fresh look to your home's entry. I just transformed my front door from black to pastel pink, and it looks fabulous!

- Front door decorative items: A front door wreath is a welcoming sign to family and friends and adds a decorative element to your front entry. Wreaths can be easily found online if you can't find them locally, and they are often inexpensive. Consider changing your front door wreath seasonally.
- Doormats: The placement of an entry mat by all the entry doors will ground the energy coming in and out of your home. Add mats with patterns and in a color that works with your front door color. Online retailers like Frontgate have great options for durable and functional solutions in several shapes and sizes.
- Pillows and throws: Pillows and throw on a sitting chair or bench are simple ways to portray a warm welcome to all your family and friends.
- Light fixtures: Replace tired outdated light fixtures with new streamlined lights in a current oil-rubbed bronze, black, copper, or nickel finish.
- Door hardware: Replace your front door hardware with a new style and finish. I recommend having the same finish for the front door hardware and front-entry light fixtures.

# Chapter 5

# COMPLETE THE TRANSFORMATION USING TRADE SECRETS

My design career has expanded over two decades, and over time, I learned a trick or two when it comes to finding the perfect solutions for a client. And I've put together some of them for you to explore and adopt into your next home project.

## Make Your Own Area Rugs

We discussed the importance of area rugs in chapter 4, and a designer's trick when you need a custom area rug is to make it using a broadloom carpet. It is an easy, cost-effective way to create an area rug exactly the size you need. There are hundreds of broadloom carpet styles, colors, and patterns to choose from, and after knowing your color palette, vision, and the feel you want to achieve, you can find endless options at your local carpet stores. Your carpet store can order you carpet samples so you can review them alongside your paint colors, furniture, and flooring at home. Once you find the perfect carpet, your carpet store can provide you with an estimate of the finished size you need. Verify that the cost includes the cutting and binding of all the edges. Most often, carpet stores either do the cutting and binding or send it out to a local supplier. Consider using a wool or synthetic surge edge detail instead of machine binding or add a carpet border around all sides in a different color carpet. Stair runners can also be made from the broadloom carpet using the same edge details as an area rug. And don't forget to have an estimate to cut a carpet pad for the area rug. A carpet pad will enhance the longevity of the area rug and provide flooring protection, especially from the sun. These details will make your area rug unique and a luxurious addition to any room.

## Another Look at Your Doors and Trims

White or a version of white is a traditional approach to painting doors and trims and can act as a frame for the windows or a contrast with the wall paint color. White doors and white trim are a de facto standard for some, but before you go and order two gallons of your favorite white color, consider painting your trim and doors in a different color that balances with the undertones of your wall paint and flooring color.

If you want to achieve a better room flow and want your room to feel larger, try applying the same wall color to all the trim and doors throughout your entire home. I have a fifteen-foot-long entry hallway with six doors and five-inch-tall baseboards all within the space. I minimized all contrasting colors of door casings and baseboard trim by painting them the same color as the walls, resulting in a hallway that flows and brings attention to my furniture and artwork instead of all the white paint on all the doors, trim, and baseboards.

Another idea is to paint both sides of your interior doors a tone lighter or darker than your flooring material, paint the backside of your front door your favorite color to act as an accent feature in your entry or add wood doors with minimal grain and a monochromatic paint color palette for a timeless feel. In my extra-long hallway, I painted all the doors a lighter color than my floor material, and it provides a subtle interest to the doors as well as balances with my flooring. If you have stained trim and doors and love the richness of the wood, consider restaining them in a lighter or darker tone that enhances your new paint color palette while still balancing with your flooring material.

If you want to achieve a modern, clean look in your home, consider removing your door trim and/or window trim. I've recommended this approach, especially for new construction or extensive remodel projects when the client wants to achieve a modern, clean aesthetic. Windows and door casings with a drywall return and minimal-height baseboards provide a jumping-off point for the simple, clean look that many desire in their homes today.

## Upper Cabinets

A current design trend is to have open shelves incorporated into a kitchen, mudroom, laundry, or office space, and I think this direction is planning on staying around for a while. I know this look is not for everyone, but it is a good option to consider when you are planning a remodel or just tired of using a step stool to reach cabinet shelves. A quick trick to get a sense of the space upper cabinets take up in a kitchen is to stand back and look at how different a room feels without any upper cabinets. Incorporating open shelves into your room provides for good energy flow and achieves a lighter feel to the entire space.

Other rooms, such as a mudroom or office, can incorporate floating or open shelves for easy access to items and to add visual interest to a wall. Tidiness is a consideration when you have items on the shelves, but more important is the energy movement and feeling you achieve by installing them.

## Beautiful Bookshelves

One of my favorite things to do as an interior designer is organizing bookcases or shelves for clients. I find joy in organizing different types of books and accessory pieces that share insights about the homeowners and are also aesthetically appealing. The arrangement of the pieces should tell a story about themselves, their families, their travels, and their hobbies and bring peace and happiness to the room. It may take several edits to get all the shelves in balance with one another and to your liking.

Some guidelines to consider include the following:

- Theme: Arrange books by theme—travel, fiction, art, or sports—which also makes them easy to find.

- Spine colors: Display similar book spines in similar colors. For example, a red-colored spine cover grouped with light, pale-colored covers will stick out and draw attention only to it and not to all the other books.
- Placement: Stack books both horizontally and vertically and according to width and height. Place the larger books on the bottom or ends and stack them toward the smaller books.
- Accessories: Display in odd numbers, preferably in threes, and in varying sizes, shapes, and textures for added interest.

## Minimize Electronics in Bedrooms

Especially in master bedrooms, the use and display of any electronics need to be eliminated or minimized. The bedroom needs to be a place of calm and a sanctuary where you can rest and refresh so you can give back to yourself, your family, your community, and the world. Electronics deplete energy in the room and project negative energy. They simply contradict what a bedroom must be used for. Watch TV in your TV room, and create a peaceful sanctuary bedroom for you to restore your body and soul.

## Spray Paint

As my painter Billy always says, anything can be painted, and I share this notion wholeheartedly. I've surprised several clients when I arrive at their homes with my spray paint in hand, ready to change a light fixture, mirror frame, ceramic pots, or outdoor metal furniture with a fresh new color. Once you've defined your new paint color palette path, explore other items inside and outside of your home that are calling for a new color, all with an inexpensive can of spray paint. You'd be surprised how quickly a can of spray paint will transform the smallest of things into perfection.

## Lampshades

Lamps are an important decorative element in any room, and the shade plays an important role in how the lamp will work in the space. The style and color of a lampshade can greatly enhance the lamp, yet sometimes when you order a lamp, you don't like the shade material or shape of the shade when you see it in person. A trick I use is to change the lampshades on different lamps, which is an easy and quick way to bring new life to a lamp. If you are still not happy with how a particular lampshade looks on a lamp, you can customize a shade to your specifications. There are several online custom lampshade suppliers that I've used, and the results bring a new look and feel to any lamp in your home.

## Bring Nature Inside

It only takes a few pieces to ground a room in the natural feel of the outdoors. Natural materials portray a calm, grounding feel to a space, and I always try to incorporate colors that are found in nature, such as soft warm blues, greens, and all ranges of off-white for my paint and fabric colors and natural warm brown taupe wood finishes. Natural materials such as rattan or jute found in furniture, lighting, or area rugs, window coverings made of natural woven weave materials, or draperies made of natural linen fabric are impactful ways to bring nature indoors. Reclaimed wood with a rustic patina look on cabinetry or furniture is a popular way to ground a room and instantly create a natural feel. Handmade baskets, wool blankets, candles, and clay pottery are just a few accessory ideas to explore to bring the outside into your new home. Greenery, whether real or faux, trees, or succulents, brings positive energy to any room, and I love working with all shapes and sizes of trees and plants. If your space has a corner that needs to be filled, consider a potted faux tree, which brings color, height, and interest to the room. Faux greens are so realistic nowadays, and there are great selections online to explore.

## Fabrics and Flooring Directions

Upholstery, drapery, and multiuse fabric contents have improved tenfold since I started in the design industry two decades ago, and technology has again improved their durability, stain and soil resistance, and color longevity capabilities for both interior and outdoor fabric contents. Fabric manufacturers blend ever-evolving synthetic and natural fiber contents and regularly release new styles and colorways. Leather or faux leather is not the only answer for a sofa or chair when you have pets or a house full of kids. Upholstery fabrics are graded for durability, and the higher the grade, the more durable the fabric contents are, and many have technological stain resistance means of incorporating materials into the fibers that are superior in resisting or removing stains. Consider changing your boring beige outdoor furniture cushions or reupholstering a sitting chair in a fresh new color, pattern, or textured fabric. The options for finding the perfect solution for your upholstery, window coverings, or accessory needs are endless.

One of the most expensive decisions you will make when doing a remodel or building a new house is the flooring material. As mentioned with other materials, technology is changing the flooring industry by leaps and bounds with improvements in durability, stain resistance, and water- and sound-proofing qualities. The overall appearance of engineered hardwoods to luxury vinyl planks (LVP), luxury vinyl tiles (LVT), and laminate flooring is realistic in not only how they look but also how they feel. Broadloom carpets with technological advances in fiber contents and weaves and expanded styles and sizes of porcelain and ceramic tiles are the directions flooring manufacturers are taking to exceed all your flooring needs. If you are not partnering with an interior designer on a flooring project, I highly recommend you partner with the staff at your local flooring retail store, as they have a wealth of knowledge on flooring manufacturers' product releases and current industry trends.

# CHAPTER 6

# LAUNCH YOUR NEW LIFE

You have finally finished your project, and it's time to sit quietly in your new home and appreciate all you've accomplished. Once you committed to your vision, you persevered through all the ebbs and flows of your project, made all the material decisions, and hopefully uncovered a hidden skill or talent set that was buried inside you. Take time to experience your personal transformation and affirm all your hard work and the beautiful creations that you can admire for years to come.

Your home is a living soul, and it needs to be taken care of as you would yourself. Living in beautiful and healthy environments has a direct impact on our lives, and studies show that your well-being is related to how you live with your home environment. You now know how color affects one's moods and emotions, and you can make paint and furnishings color selections based on how you want to feel and what mood you want to convey.

> "The field of mind-body studies includes research on the relationship between our surroundings and our health. Studies show that a healthy and pleasing environment, like plants in your office, or a treasured photograph on the wall, can do more than simply improve your mood—it can affect your immune system and physical health." (Louise Delagran, MA, MEd)

I hope that you incorporate some of the simple changes that are outlined in the book, which may very well improve your health and well-being.

Throughout the book, I discussed the energy of a house and the importance of feeling a space. Whether I am a team member on an extensive remodel or new build or I oversee my own remodel project, it's a good idea to clear out everyone's energy from your new home so that your energy will permeate within it. Burning sage is one of the oldest and purest methods of cleansing a space, and it's important to do this once all the workers have finished the project and are no longer in your house. Why would you want other people's energy in your home and not your own? I burn dried sage wands and walk the entire house from room to room to release bad or negative energy and allow good energy to enter each space. I also burn sage in clients' homes when there is negative or bad energy associated with them or with the house, such as death. One of my favorite gifts for clients is a sage gift box, which includes sage wands, clearing crystals, and some books on sage rituals. Most sage gifts can be found on Etsy or other online suppliers.

You've achieved your goal by creating a transformation roadmap, and now it's time to celebrate. I hope you've found a sense of accomplishment and a can-do spirit to propel you on to your next home project. Your willingness to transform your house into a home has led you to a new place within. Cherish the new you and your new beginning in your Authentic Home.

# References

## Chapter 1

Feng Shui, Google search.
Houzz is an American website online community and software for architecture, interior design and decorating, landscape design, and home improvement. Houzz Ideabooks are a place where you can store ideas and build dreams.
Next Door, Angie's List, Google search.
National Association of Productivity and Organization Professional, Google search.
California Closets, Garage Experts custom closet organization companies, Google search.
Color Moods, Google search.

## Chapter 2

Kondo, Marie. *The Life-Changing Magic of Tidying Up: The Japanese Art of Decluttering and Organizing.*

## Chapter 3

Color properties and Characteristics, Google search.
The Spruce. *Choosing a Color Schemes from the Color Wheel.*
Sherwin-Williams paint manufacturer.

## Chapter 4

Home Goods, At Home, and Pottery Barn are home décor retail stores.
Hunter Douglas, Horizons, and the Shade Store are window covering manufacturers.
Lighting. Google search.
Visual Comfort, Arteriors Home, and Hudson Valley are lighting manufacturers.
Frontgate is a home décor retailer.

## Chapter 6

Louise Delagran, MA, MEd. *Taking Charge of Your Health and Wellbeing*. Etsy is a global marketplace of unique and creative goods.

# About the Author

Kathy, a designer, color consultant, and entrepreneur, has lovingly transformed hundreds of homes over two decades in both the Pacific Northwest and New England states. She currently resides in Coeur d'Alene, Idaho, with her husband, Rick.

Printed in the USA
CPSIA information can be obtained
at www.ICGtesting.com
LVHW051031240824
789170LV00008BA/134